More
Surprise Sketches

by Ronald Rich

Twelve Sketches for Church or Conference

No performance of these sketches may be given without the written permission of the publisher to whom all applications for performing rights should be made, enclosing a reply paid envelope, to the National Christian Education Council.

Published by:
National Christian Education Council
1020 Bristol Road
Selly Oak
Birmingham
B29 6LB

Published for:
RADIUS
Christ Church and Upton Chapel
Kennington Road
London
SE1 7PQ

British Library Cataloguing-in-Publication data:
A catalogue record for this book is available from the British Library.

ISBN 0-7197-0865-6

A co-operative venture in Christian Drama by NCEC and RADIUS.

RADIUS is the shortened name of the Religious Drama Society of Great Britain, bringing together amateur and professional actors, writers, and others involved in religion and the performing arts.

RADIUS exists to encourage all drama which throws light on the human condition, especially through a Christian understanding. It aims to help local congregations towards a deeper appreciation of all types of drama, to inform them of opportunities to see work of a high quality, to give the technical advice and assistance needed for a good standard of local productions, and to help them find ways of introducing the lively arts into their worship.

The society runs a unique lending library, organises an annual summer school, holds regular play-writing competitions and publishes its own magazine.

First published 1995
© Ronald Rich 1995

Typesetting by Kirsteen Williams, National Christian Education Council.
Printed and bound by Street & Co Ltd, Baldock, Hertfordshire.

CONTENTS

THIS IS THE DAY

Production Note: *A child and an elderly person, who is carrying a Bible, walk together to the centre. They stop. (The characters can be male or female.)*

CHILD	Can you answer me a question, Grandpa?
GRANDPA	I'll try. What is it?
CHILD	People keep telling me that I am the Church of tomorrow - but I'm here *now*.
GRANDPA	I know. Somebody told me I am a 'has been' - I am the Church of yesterday - but I'm here now.
CHILD	So - who is the Church of today, Grandpa?
GRANDPA	I don't know, but I know a man who does. Let's ask him.

> *GRANDPA opens the Bible and they look into it together. The CHILD excitedly points to a text.*

CHILD	*(Reads)* Jesus Christ is the same yesterday.
GRANDPA	*(Serenely confident)* I know.

> *CHILD looks up at GRANDPA and pats him on the back. GRANDPA looks again at the Bible. He points to the text.*

	And tomorrow.
CHILD	Hooray!

> *GRANDPA pats CHILD on the head.*

GRANDPA	*(Looking again at the Bible)* And *today.*

> *GRANDPA closes Bible*

CHILD	So what's the answer, Grandpa? Who is the Church of today?
GRANDPA	We are!

> *They slap palms and walk off together, GRANDPA'S arm around CHILD'S shoulder.*

Talking Point

As a society we tend to exclude the very young and the elderly. Are Christians also guilty of this? Are there other groups of people who might feel excluded from the Church? What can we do to make them feel that they belong?

LOST FOR WORDS

Production Note: *A man (A) and a woman (B) are sitting on chairs, centre stage.*

A   It's you and me, then. I hoped it would be.

B   Thank you, kind sir. To be honest, I don't much like this bit. *(Quotes)* 'Everybody turn and talk to your neighbour.' Lots of people find that acutely embarrassing.

A   Oh, I don't know. That's what makes a conference come alive. *(Points forward)* Look at them, all talking to each other. Getting really close. Down to brass tacks.

B   Whatever that means.

Pause.

A   It's no good just sitting down side by side and never really relating to those around you. There's a kind of natural barrier between people.

B   That's what I like. A bit of space. It's what makes us individuals.

A   It's no good everybody being a little island is it? Notices up all round saying, 'Don't come any nearer'.

B   *(Dismissive)* Hmm.

Pause. B looks at her watch. Pause.

B   So - what do we talk about?

A   Anything. He said we could talk about anything.

B   Anything?

A   Yes.

B   All right then, you start.

A   No, go on - you.

B   What do you want to know about me?

A   Whatever you want to tell me.

B   Like what?

A   Anything.

B   *(Pause)* I can't *think* of anything. You start.

A   Oh, all right. *(Thinks - unsuccessfully)* It's hard, isn't it?

B	Yes.
A	It's no good. I can't think of anything either.
B	You're not trying.
A	I am.
B	You see, it's a waste of time. Admit it.
A	No it isn't. It's *us*. We're just not relating. *(Looks round)* I think he's calling everybody together. *(Stands)* Come on.
B	I hope we don't have to report back. *(Stands)*
A	No, all this is private.
B	What is?
A	Whatever passed between us.
B	But nothing did!
A	Nevertheless, it remains confidential. *(Begins to walk off)*
B	That's good. *(Smiling)* It wouldn't do for everyone to know that we've been married twenty years and can't find anything to say.

Exits.

Talking Point

Communicating with others can be difficult, particularly within the family. Are we shying away from something that is vital for our well-being? Do we find it easy to communicate with God? As individuals? As a Church?

AT YOUR SERVICE

CHARACTERS

HUSBAND	)	Looking for a good meal
WIFE	)	
WAITER		Eager to serve

Production Note: A table is set centre stage with tablecloth, plates, cruet, etc. A sign on the back wall reads 'Ecclesia Restaurant'. A HUSBAND and WIFE enter and after a moment of indecision, choose the table and sit down. A WAITER appears with a long, white apron tied at the waist. He has a cloth over his arm and he carries two menus.

WAITER	*(Brightly)* Good morning.
BOTH	Good morning.

The WAITER hands them menus.

HUSBAND	*(Complains)* There was no-one at the door to greet us.
WAITER	Tut, tut. Well you didn't have far to walk, did you?
HUSBAND	*(Not appeased)* I suppose it's all right to sit here?
WAITER	Yes, perfectly all right. You can sit anywhere.
HUSBAND	But it says 'Reserved' over there *(Pointing)*, *and* there.
WAITER	Ah, yes, well we have regular customers who always *insist* on sitting in the same place. Woe betide anyone who sits there first. Ha! Ha!

HUSBAND and WIFE join in. The WAITER'S laughter stops abruptly.

WAITER	Otherwise you can sit anywhere.
WIFE	*(Pointing)* Apart from...

WAITER	Of course. Now - what would you like to order?

HUSBAND and WIFE study their menus.

WIFE	I'm not very hungry.
WAITER	May I suggest the hymn sandwich?
HUSBAND	*(Sotto voce to WIFE)* Boring.
WAITER	*(Urging)* A lot of our customers like the hymn sandwich. They ask for it again and again. It's very popular.
HUSBAND	No imagination.
WAITER	What?
HUSBAND	I can imagine.
WIFE	*(Pointing to her menu)* What's this 'stew'?
WAITER	It's a stew, madam.
WIFE	I know *that*, but what's *in* it?
WAITER	Almost anything.
WIFE	Anything? You mean like warmed-up leftovers?
WAITER	Well...
HUSBAND	*(Pointing to his menu)* Second time round?
WAITER	It's the chef's special, sir.
HUSBAND	I'll bet it is.
WIFE	I fancy something meaty today.
WAITER	You'll be lucky.
WIFE	What?
WAITER	You're lucky, madam. There's a special offer. *(He indicates on her menu)* Here.
WIFE	*(Reads)* 'Really solid food.' *(To HUSBAND)* That sounds interesting.
HUSBAND	It's a long time since we had *that*.
WIFE	Might be indigestible, though. Can you recommend it?
WAITER	Oh, yes, madam.
HUSBAND	What exactly does it consist of?
WAITER	Strong meat, sir. For people who mean business. We only have it now and then.
HUSBAND	Strong meat, eh? I think I'll have some of that. How about you?

WIFE	I don't know. *(Pointing to her menu)* What's this - 'hot pot'?
	Puzzled, the WAITER looks at her menu and wipes it with his cloth.
WAITER	No, that's hotch potch, madam. That's a regular item here.
WIFE	Oh? And what's in that?
WAITER	A bit of everything. Suits everyone - children, pensioners, gourmets, McDonald's brigade, Egon Ronay, Arthur Daley... Would you like that, madam? Goes down well. No after-effects.
HUSBAND	*(Approvingly to WIFE)* No after-effects, dear.
WAITER	*(Very positively)* None whatsoever.
WIFE	We're thinking of bringing the grandchildren. Have you anything suitable for them?
WAITER	*(Enthusiastically)* I should think we have! Tailor-made for their young palates. Sweet and gooey. Nothing stringy or tough. Easy to swallow.
WIFE	*(Looking at her menu)* Where does it say all that?
WAITER	Oh, they don't eat here with you. They're in a room upstairs. They have a menu of their own.
HUSBAND	But we want them to eat here with *us*.
WAITER	Well, if you insist. In that case I recommend the hotch potch.
HUSBAND	I've noticed you relay music during your meals.
WAITER	Oh, yes. Some of our customers come specially for the music.
WIFE	What sort of music do you play?
WAITER	Old classics. Traditional mostly. Lots of Victoriana. Great tunes.
WIFE	*(To HUSBAND)* That's good.
WAITER	Laced with some hot little modern numbers, of course. Got to keep up with the times.
HUSBAND	Supposing people don't like them?
WAITER	*(Surprised)* Don't like them?
HUSBAND	The - 'hot little numbers'.
WAITER	They can always complain.
HUSBAND	Do they?
WAITER	No.

WIFE	They are obviously satisfied.
HUSBAND	Or tone deaf.
WIFE	I see you do candlelight dinners with flambeau cooking.
WAITER	A speciality, sir. Very romantic. Discerning diners swear by it.
HUSBAND	You mean the good food?
WAITER	Not so much that, sir, it's the candles, and the smoke. *(Smiles at the recollection)* Makes them come over all peaceful.
HUSBAND	Well I think we'd better order, dear.
WIFE	I really don't think I want anything after all.
HUSBAND	Well, if you aren't eating, I think I'll give it a miss too.

HUSBAND and WIFE stand.

WAITER	*(Dismayed)* What - nothing?
HUSBAND	Sorry.

HUSBAND and WIFE move towards exit.

WAITER	*(Hopefully)* If you come back tomorrow, it's gala night. We 'sing along' all through the meal. Good old chorus stuff. Goes a treat.
HUSBAND	*(Politely)* No, thank you.
WAITER	*(Desperate)* What about our 'special' next week? Everybody gets involved. Some even go in the kitchen to help the chef. And after the main course everyone goes round hugging everyone else. Tremendous fun.
HUSBAND	Not really. Not 'us', is it dear?
WIFE	Can you recommend the place down the road?
WAITER	*(Grudgingly)* You mean St Grub's Cafe? Oh, yes. Why not? They have a small, regular clientele. Keep coming back - so I'm told.
HUSBAND	A good menu, I expect.
WAITER	Hardly, sir. Just one dish, you see. It's the same every week at St Grub's.
HUSBAND	*(Surprised)* Really? *(Wanting to praise it)* Reliable, then.
WAITER	Like clockwork.
HUSBAND	Well, thank you. We must think about all this.

| WAITER | That's right, sir. |

HUSBAND and WIFE move to door.

| WIFE | Oh, by the way. Do you make a service charge? |
| WAITER | Gracious no, madam. The service is free. But there *is* a plate at the door. |

HUSBAND and WIFE exit swiftly. WAITER flicks a speck of dust off the table and exits.

Talking Point

It is never easy to please everybody. Where do our priorities lie? Where should they lie?

KNOCK, KNOCK!

CHARACTERS

A and B	House visitors, enthusiastic but nervous
FIRST MAN	No time for door salesmen
WOMAN	Housewife, no time to spare, busy
SECOND MAN	Courteous, interested
THIRD MAN	Bright and welcoming

Production Note: Four chairs are placed in line from L to R a metre apart with their backs to the audience. Each chair is occupied. Two people (A and B) enter, each is carrying a Bible. They slowly approach the chairs from downstage.

A	House to house. It's an old, tried and tested means of evangelism.
B	Out among the people. Gives you a glow, doesn't it?
A	Yes. *(Takes a deep breath of pleasure)* The market place.

They reach the first chair.

B	You can start.
A	*(Gives way very politely)* It's all right.
B	No, go on. *(Pause)* You see, I'm a bit new at it.
A	Well, so am I. Does it actually work?
B	Of course it does. *(Pause)* Now and then. *(Urging)* Go on.
A	It doesn't look a very promising street. If we went to...
B	Go ON!

A knocks on the door. The seated figure rises and comes to the front (ie back) of his chair. He is suspicious and curt.

FIRST MAN	Yes?
A	Do you want your roof insulated?
FIRST MAN	What?

A	Or your garden tools sharpened?
FIRST MAN	No!
A	Double glazing?

The FIRST MAN swiftly resumes his seat.

B	*(Amazed)* What did you say all that for?
A	I was paralysed.
B	Garden tools sharpened?
A	I don't know what came over me.
B	*(Incredulous)* Double glazing!!

B pushes in front of A.

B	Here, let me.

B knocks at the next door. It is opened by a WOMAN. She has washing-up gloves on.

WOMAN	What do you want? Hurry up, I'm busy.
B	Er... do you want your carpets shampooed?

WOMAN swiftly resumes her seat.

B	*(But too late)...* Your car washed?
A	Terrific! That'll pull them in. Chairs down the aisles.
B	It isn't easy. I was...
A	Paralysed. I know. But why? What are we afraid of?
B	Nothing.
A	Right.
B	*(Determined)* Right.
A	Well then, let's try again - together.

They move to the next house. A knocks at the door. A SECOND MAN steps in front of his chair.

SECOND MAN *(Pleasantly)* Morning.

A	Good morning. Can you give us a minute to tell you what we believe?
B	And why we think it's the greatest message in the world?
SECOND MAN	OK. Sure.
B	What!
SECOND MAN	I'm listening.
A	I knew you wouldn't. *(To B)* Didn't I say... *(Double take)* You're listening?
SECOND MAN	All ears.
B	That's remarkable. That *is* remarkable.
A	Do you know, nine people out of ten don't want to know.
SECOND MAN	Really?
A	Just aren't interested. Couldn't care less. I was saying to my friend...
B	They just shut the door. Won't even give you a minute.
A	It's true.
B	Deaf to everything.
A	Deaf.

SECOND MAN looks at his watch.

A	You get used to it, of course. All part of the job.

SECOND MAN resumes his seat unnoticed by A and B who are now really talking to each other.

B	But it can be a bit wearing, can't it? Door after door after door...
A	Absolutely, but - we plough on, don't we?
B	Yes, we do.
A	*(Turns back to man)* So you can imagine our surprise...
B	He's gone!
A	Typical. You see? *(Pause)* It's tragic.

They move away.

A	Well, there you are. Nine out of ten. Wouldn't you know! It's *just* what I expected.
B	*(Pause)* Maybe that's the trouble.

A	What d'you mean?
B	We got what we expected.
A	I don't follow.
B	Think about it. Come on, let's start again. *(Urges)* Have a bit of faith.
A	Right. Leave this to me. I've got a feeling about this one.

A knocks on the fourth chair. A THIRD MAN stands up and comes to the front of his chair. He wears a clerical collar. He holds an open Bible.

THIRD MAN   *(Cheerfully)* Good morning!

A and B stare at him then quickly turn their faces towards each other with a look of surprise. They look back at the THIRD MAN.

Talking Point

In totally unpredictable situations everyone is apprehensive, but why do we lack confidence when asked to witness to our faith? What are the links, if any, between self-confidence and faith?

RAW MATERIAL

A   *(To audience, smugly)* In our worship drama this morning I shall be playing the part of St Peter.

B   You needn't sound as though you were type-cast for the part.

A   What do you mean?

B   *(Mimics)* 'I shall be playing the part of St Peter.' *(Pause)* Nobody else offered, did they?

A   That's nothing to do with it.

B   Of course it is! If there was a choice we wouldn't have been chosen.

A   Thank you!

B   Well, let's face it. We just had to have whoever was available.

A   Aren't you forgetting something?

B   What's that?

A   Oh, just a tiny, tiny thing called talent.

B   All right, then, I'll include it.

A   Thank you.

B   Your tiny, tiny talent.

A   Now, look here... !

B   In Oberammergau...

A   We are not *in* Oberammergau.

B   In Oberammergau, the actor playing St Peter lives the part for a couple of years beforehand. Grows a beard...

A   *(Objecting)* I'm not growing a beard!

B   ...and he has to be like St Peter - every day, not just look like him. The Virgin Mary has to be a saintly woman, and so on. And as for Jesus, well...

A   Oh you'd do that part to perfection, I'm sure!

B   All I'm saying is...

A   That you don't think I'm right for the part.

B shrugs his shoulders.

Well, I'm not the only one. What about these other parts? I mean to say!

B	There's no need to get excited. Such as what?
A	*(Reads from the script)* Pilate - 'a man of haughty manner and imposing stature.' That's what it says.
B	So?
A	And you suggested Arthur Bennett? I ask you!
B	Why not? He has a haughty manner.
A	Pompous, I'd call it.
B	And an imposing stature.
A	Imposing? He's just fat. And the last time he did any acting, he was a sunflower in the Primary School pageant.
B	I heard he was very good.

A looks at his script again.

A	Then there's the 'little serving maid' - *(Looks up with incredulity)* Mrs Pilling? Come on - do me a favour!
B	She's a good actress.
A	She'll have to be to take the part of a 'little serving maid' - she's eighty!
B	Well, she looks young for her age.
A	*(Pause)* And what about you?
B	*(Bridling)* What about me?
A	Caiaphas?
B	That's right.
A	*(Reading from script)* 'Devious, shifty, hypocritical...'
B	It's a great challenge. I'll have to put a lot into it.
A	*(Surveying him)* Oh, I don't know.
B	All right, you've made your point. Choosing the right team isn't easy - not from our lot.
A	No. And we're not the first to have trouble with it. Jesus wanted someone to lead the disciples after he had gone, remember? Someone strong, dependable, loyal, rock-like. What did he get?
B	Peter.
A	Exactly. More like shifting sand.
B	...who denied him in the end.
B	Yes, and what about the others? Were they any better?
A	Not a lot... He wanted a strong team round him who would be faithful friends as well as disciples. What did he get?

19

B	Men who argued among themselves about who was the greatest, and ran away when the crunch came.
A	Right. And when he wanted someone to look after their money and the gifts people gave them for the poor - what happened?
B	He got Judas.
A	Betrayal, that's what he got! There was no way he could make a success out of that scenario.
B	But he did! Even with them.
A	There you are, then. We all have to work with what we get, don't we? *(Looking piously upwards)* Even He does!
B	Yes, He has to put up with you, for a start.

A looks affronted. B quickly corrects himself.

	I mean 'us'. So, let's get on with the drama, shall we?
A	Right.
B	You're Peter.
A	Well, thank you.
B	Not at all.
A	And Pilate - a bit on the stout side, then?
B	*(Generously)* Why not?
A	And you're still Caiaphas?
B	'Devious and shifty'? - right. *(Warning)* I'll have to act my socks off.
A	*(Conceding)* Of course! And 'the little serving maid' - Mrs Pilling - agreed?
B	*(Doubtful)* We-e-ll... *(They both laugh)* agreed!

They shake hands, and cast a look heavenward.

A and B	Over to you, Lord!

They exit.

Talking Point

God accepts us as we are. He doesn't wait until we are perfect but takes the raw material and begins his work. Should this affect the way we treat other people? Does it?

MY HEART GOES OUT TO YOU

Production Note: *Two church officials are centre stage quietly talking. They are B and C. A third official, A, joins them and interrupts their conversation. They are all friends. It is important that the group of three stays fairly close together, almost conspiratorially.*

A	*(Anxiously)* Can I have a word? There's a chap in the porch.
B	In the porch? What sort of chap? Who is it?
A	I found him at the back of the church after the service asking for money.
C	Oh, dear. What did you tell him?
A	I asked him to wait. Thought I'd come along and see you first. You are on duty.
B	*(Void of ideas)* What do you want us to do?
C	We've had this sort of thing before. What did he say?
A	He said he wants some money - for a bite to eat.
C	A drop to drink, more like it.
A	*(Defensively)* Well, we don't know that, do we?
B	What's his story?
A	Story?
B	Yes, there's always a story. I expect he'll say he's got a job to go to tomorrow and he's travelled from somewhere or other to get here. Used up all his money. Just needs something to keep him going till he gets his job. Something like that.
C	Aren't there benefits these days? All these chaps can get them, can't they?
A	Not on Sundays. Anyway, he needs an address to qualify and he hasn't got one yet.
B	*(Dismissively)* Classic.
C	If you help him, they'll all be round here.
A	Who will?
C	I don't know. *(Pause)* Was he at the service?
A	No.

B	Well, there you are.
C	How much does he want?
A	He didn't say.

Pause.

B	Well, we've got to lock up. Where is he now?
A	In the porch.
C	Look, *(Searches trouser pockets)* I've got about...
B	No, no. I don't think so. I mean, this could happen every Sunday, couldn't it?
A	But it doesn't, does it?

C replaces the loose change.

B	*(Insisting)* There might be half a dozen of them next week. Word gets round.
C	*(Desperate)* We can't just do nothing.
B	Yes we can. They shouldn't be encouraged. Not in my view. Big, is he? Strong, aggressive?
A	No, a bit thin, really.
B	Ah.

Pause.

A	*(Trying out the idea)* I suppose I could invite him to dinner.
B	What! Take him home, you mean?
A	I'd have to ask the family first, of course.
B	I don't think that's a good idea at all.
C	Bit of a risk. What does he look like? I mean, you never know, do you?
B	You'd never get rid of him.
C	Risky.
B	*(Decides)* I shouldn't do anything. That's the best thing.
A	Makes you feel rather - guilty though, doesn't it?
B	Guilty? What - you? After all you've done for the church? Guilty? Never. No, look *(As though explaining to a small child)* - I'd be quite firm and say, 'Sorry, we just don't give out money at the church door.'
C	That's reasonable.

B	It is.
C	And it's true.
B	That's right.
A	*(Hesitantly)* Well, all right... would you like to go and... ?
B	No, I don't think so. Well, you've met him, haven't you? He knows you.

A looks appealingly at C who simply shakes his (or her) head.

A	*(Reluctantly)* All right, then. I'll go.

A leaves.

B	They put you on the spot these people. I thought it was dying out.
C	They do it on purpose, of course. Think we're an easy touch. I suppose it's a compliment, really.
B	Compliment?
C	Well, they probably reckon that we're more understanding than most people - have a soft spot for the poor and so on. Try to help people down on their luck. That sort of thing. Well it is the Church's message, isn't it? So to speak.

They look at each other uneasily.

B	*(Uncomfortably)* Yes, well...
C	In a way.
B	Of course.

A returns and joins them.

B	*(Cheerfully)* All settled?
A	All settled.
C	He's gone, then?
A	Yes, he's gone.
B	Thank goodness for that. *(Anxiously)* You didn't give him anything?
A	No. I didn't give him anything.

23

C	Good.
A	Mrs Hartley did.
B	What! But she hasn't got two halfpennies to rub together.
A	I know. *(Pause)* Will you lock up, then? I'll be off.

A exits.

C	*(Piously)* I did offer. You remember.
B	You did, yes... sort of. *(Pause)* If you take that door, I'll lock this one...

They move in opposite directions. C turns at the last moment.

C	*(Defensively)* I was prepared to do something.
A	'Course you were. We all were - if it came down to it. That's what counts. Heart in the right place, eh? See you tonight, then? On with the good work.

They exit.

Talking Point

Compassion is not enough: we must actively help those in need. Are Christians leading the way in this?

BACK TO BASICS

Two people meet centre stage

A   Have I got news for you!

B   Oh?

A   I'm thinking of starting a new Church. Will you join it?

B   What's wrong with the old one?

A   There - you said it. It's too old.

B   You must be joking.

A   No, I'm not. The Church is far too old to reform. Best to start afresh and get it right.

B   I see. I expect you want to throw out all the difficult bits.

A   *And* all the wrong bits.

B   Who decides they're wrong?

A   I do.

B   So the Church is going to be yours?

A   Yes. No! I just don't like it as it is. I want to start again.

B   You can't.

A   Yes I can. Other people have started Churches. It's nothing new.

B   I know, they tried it in Corinth a long time ago. You'll have to have the same Gospel.

A   Of course, goes without saying.

B   Same Bible.

A   Naturally. I'm not stupid.

B   Congregational worship?

A   Obviously.

B   The great hymns, Wesley, Watts, Cowper...

A   Can't beat 'em.

B   Baptism, Confirmation, Communion?

A   All those - of course.

B   Ministers?

A   Why not?

B   You'll want to be evangelical?

A	Absolutely.
B	Concerned for the poor and the oppressed?
A	One hundred per cent.
B	Hot against social injustice?
A	Just watch me.
B	Institutional corruption?
A	Like a ton of bricks.
B	Sounds good.
A	*(Pleased with himself)* It does, doesn't it? I thought you'd like it. Will you join?
B	I don't think so.
A	Why ever not?
B	Because I'm already a member.
A	What?
B	And, listen, I've got news for you. You're a member too.

They walk off still talking.

A	I'm talking about *my* Church.

They stop and face each other.

B	And mine
A	But I want it made new!
B	So, why not join me?

B walks off.

A	Well, if you put it like that...

B holds out his hand. They slap palms in agreement. B exits followed by A.

Talking Point

Hardly anyone is satisfied with everything as it is. Change is a key word for all that is living, including the Church. Can change for its own sake be good? Where should the impulse for change come from?

26

BEYOND THE PAGE

CHARACTERS

ASSISTANT	Eager to agree and to sell
CUSTOMER	Knows what he wants
TWO HELPERS	

Production Note: CUSTOMER and ASSISTANT are on stage. On a table is a rolled map of the world. Pinned up, facing the audience, is the famous Meteorological Office picture of the world taken from space by Meteosat - 2.

CUSTOMER	I want to buy a map.
ASSISTANT	Yes, sir. For which part of the world?
CUSTOMER	All of it. *(Looks at poster)* What about this one?
ASSISTANT	That's just a picture, sir. Taken from a satellite, 20,000 miles up. Gorgeous, isn't it? *(Becomes romantic)* A blue and white fluffy ball, floating in a black sky. Fifty-seven million square miles.
CUSTOMER	And a half.
ASSISTANT	What?
CUSTOMER	Fifty-seven *and a half* million.
ASSISTANT	Well... if you're being precise...
CUSTOMER	Don't leave that bit out! It might be where *you* live.
ASSISTANT	*(Enters the joke)* Of course! Beautiful, isn't it?
CUSTOMER	... snow-capped mountains, plains and deserts...
ASSISTANT	Farms and fields...
CUSTOMER	Forests and oceans... beautiful.
ASSISTANT	*(Enraptured)* Beautiful!
CUSTOMER	And ugly.
ASSISTANT	What?
CUSTOMER	Ugly. Maps don't tell you everything. Where's the ugliness? Oppression is ugly, malnutrition, famine and disease are ugly.
ASSISTANT	*(Capturing the spirit)* ...Ugly, ugly... greed and... and... violence... and poverty too. Very ugly, sir.

CUSTOMER ...To say nothing of illiteracy, racism, environmental rape and civil war.

They look at the picture.

...That's where we live.

ASSISTANT *(Hasn't quite got the idea yet)* Beautiful, isn't it?

CUSTOMER *(Not at all sure)* Mmm.

ASSISTANT You'll take it?

CUSTOMER No. Anyway, that's only half the picture. Doesn't show the other side. I want to see all of it.

ASSISTANT Ah! You want a mercator's projection. *(Calls to offstage)* Can you two give me a hand?

> *Two HELPERS come on and a map is unrolled. It is the usual mercator version of the world map (a simple line-drawing would do). The map should be about 4' x 3' to register with the audience. HELPERS 1 and 2 and the assistant all stand behind the map holding it up in front of their faces. The ASSISTANT in the middle.*

CUSTOMER That's the whole world?

ASSISTANT *(From behind the map)* Absolutely. Yes, sir.

CUSTOMER Absolutely **no**, sir.

The map is temporarily lowered to chest-level.

ASSISTANT What?

CUSTOMER It still doesn't tell me what I ought to know.

ASSISTANT I assure you, sir...

Customer raises map again, obscuring their faces.

It's only one-dimensional. No body to it. You could stick a pin almost anywhere in that map and you would discover all kinds of human need. Did you know that? *(Pause)* Can you hear me?

ASSISTANT *(From behind map)* Yes, sir.

28

Customer mimes taking a pin from his lapel. He tests it on his finger. He approaches the map.

CUSTOMER   Almost anywhere.

He waves the pin about then sticks it in the map.

HELPER 1   *(Loudly from behind map)* Owch!
CUSTOMER   *(Pleased)* Mmm.

He sticks the pin in again.

HELPER 2   *(From behind map, even, louder)* Owch!
CUSTOMER   *(Triumphant)* Ah, hah!

He sticks the pin in again.

ASSISTANT   *(Louder still)* OWCH!
CUSTOMER   Now, that's something *like* a map!

The map is lowered to chest-level and three rueful faces are seen.

                  I'll take it. By the way, who shouted first?
HELPER 1   I did!
CUSTOMER   That was a tea plantation in Sri Lanka.
HELPER 1   Well, it hurt.
CUSTOMER   *(Pleased)* I know. *(Pause)* Who shouted next?
HELPER 2   I did.
CUSTOMER   *(Looks at map)* That was a shanty town in Brasilia.
HELPER 2   *(Objects)* But it was me as well!
CUSTOMER   How very true!

Pause.

ASSISTANT   *(Offended)* I got pricked too, you know.
CUSTOMER   Yes - that was Tyneside, one of the highest unemployment blackspots in the country.

29

The three assistants let down the map further in front of them.

CUSTOMER   I'll take this one.

The HELPERS roll up the map and give it to the CUSTOMER. They walk off. The CUSTOMER pays the ASSISTANT.

CUSTOMER   You can keep your pretty blue and white ball. It's too far off. And it's too fuzzy. This one's more like it. I can see the places, recognise the names. It's more *human*. And, you know something else?
ASSISTANT   What's that, sir?
CUSTOMER   *(Moving off)* It's pin sharp!

CUSTOMER strides off right. ASSISTANT looks at the poster, shakes his head and walks off left, rubbing his pin-pricked chest.

Talking Point

It has been said that nothing is real until it is local. It is when we feel the sorrows of others that we are ready to act. Do events in far off places move us? Should we become more involved? If so, how?

DON'T GET CARRIED AWAY

Production Note: *Six people file on to the stage from L in order of height, the shortest first. They face the audience in a straight line, and are serious in expression throughout the sketch except where directed to smile. The tallest person speaks first, the second tallest next, and so on down the line. A pause of one second should be kept between each speaker. The first five speak with a touch of pride and confidence, but this should not be overdone.*

VOICE 1   I have the gift of friendship.
VOICE 2   I have the gift of humour.
VOICE 3   I have the gift of music.
VOICE 4   I have the gift of speaking.
VOICE 5   I have the gift of craftsmanship.

> *Slightly longer pause.*

VOICE 6   *(Not seeking our sympathy)* I have no gift at all.

> *They all remain looking steadfastly to the front, and without expression. Each one now takes a step forward before speaking, eventually forming a new line.*

VOICE 1   I have the gift of friendship. Everyone I meet becomes my friend. People take to me and love me. *(Smiles)*
VOICE 2   I have the gift of humour. I cheer up every group I enter. Soon everyone is happy and laughing. People like to have me around. *(Smiles)*
VOICE 3   I have the gift of music. I can play most instruments. The choir rely upon me. I have perfect pitch. *(Smiles)*
VOICE 4   I have the gift of speaking. I was born with a silver tongue. It is no trouble to me to stand up in front of an audience and talk about - anything. *(Smiles)*
VOICE 5   I have the gift of craftsmanship. I am good with my hands. I can

31

make something out of nothing. My initials should have been DIY. It all comes so easy. *(Smiles)*

> *Sixth speaker also takes a step forward. The previous speakers' smiles all disappear.*

> *Pause.*

VOICE 6   I have no gift at all. *(Does not smile)*

> *While remaining perfectly still, they all simultaneously turn their heads and look along the line to the R. SIX continues to look to the front, and totally impassive. The rest look simultaneously to the front again. They now speak piously and pompously.*

VOICE 1   Everyone has been given a gift.

> *Exits L.*

VOICE 2   No-one has been left out.

> *Exits R.*

VOICE 3   Every gift is different.

> *Exits L.*

VOICE 4   Every gift is needed.

> *Exits R.*

VOICE 5   *(With a swift glance at SIX)* The person without a gift simply doesn't exist.

> *Exits L.*

> *Pause.*

VOICE 6   I have no gift at all. *(Slightly longer pause)* I don't exist.

> *SIX quickly pulls out a large plain paper bag from under his coat and puts it over his head, as ONE and THREE enter from L and, one on each side, take SIX by the elbows lifting him an inch or two off the ground, and carry him off R.*

Talking Point

What is the difference between humility and self-devaluation? All the characters in this sketch have something to learn: God has surely gifted us all.

DO YOU READ ME?

CHARACTERS

HUSBAND   Reluctant churchgoer
WIFE   Regular churchgoer
PREACHER   Popular Minister
MEMBERS OF THE CONGREGATION

Production Note: Several people are represented as sitting in pews at a church service. This can be achieved by placing chairs close together, diagonally in relation to the audience. Two people are seated on the front chairs, and two, three, or four in the row behind. In front of them all is a lectern behind which stands the PREACHER. The characters on the front row are HUSBAND and WIFE. Only they and the PREACHER have speaking parts. On each occasion when a character reveals his or her inner thoughts a rectangular card bearing the word THINKS becomes visible just above his head. This card is on the end of a stick and is raised unobtrusively by the person sitting behind the speaker. The card for the PREACH-ER is activated by himself. This could be attached to the lectern, visible, but presenting its blind side to the audience until unobtrusively twisted by the PREACHER. When a character is revealing his or her inner thoughts, all the other participants are oblivious of what is being said and studiously pay attention to the PREACHER.

Alternatively, instead of using cards and sticks, the character can turn towards the audience while revealing his or her inner thoughts. The other characters should remain attentive to the PREACHER.

WIFE   I wish you wouldn't make it so obvious that you didn't want to come to church.

HUSBAND   What have I done now?

WIFE   You're staring at your feet. It's obvious. You always do that when you're bored.

HUSBAND   *(With a nod towards the lectern)* But he doesn't know that. Anyway, why did we have to come to the very front row?

WIFE   We were shown to this pew, weren't we? It's a busy church. He's a popular preacher.

HUSBAND	We'll soon see.

He begins to fiddle with books.

	I shall never find my way through these. I hope he announces the page numbers.
PREACHER	Will you turn to page 45.
HUSBAND	Well done.
WIFE	Ssh!
PREACHER	The Lord be with you.
WIFE	And also with you.
HUSBAND	What was that page again?
PREACHER	Psalms 62 and 41.

Everyone stands, HUSBAND follows.

WIFE	*(Thinks)* **I think this might be a difficult service. He's determined not to do anything right. I know the signs.**

She turns to look at HUSBAND. He smiles at her. She smiles back. She looks across the church.

Good Heavens, whatever has Mrs Gosling got on her head?! I'm sure I saw that at the Bring and Buy yesterday. And there's the butcher... It must be six months since *he* was here last... I want a word with him about the scrag-end he sold me on Wednesday. Disgraceful.

They sit.

WIFE	*(Hissing)* Stop fiddling with the change in your pocket.
HUSBAND	What happens now?
PREACHER	The morning offerings will now be received.
HUSBAND	I thought he wouldn't forget that! Bang goes my loose change.
WIFE	Good! You'll have nothing left to rattle.
HUSBAND	*(Thinks)* **This must be the only place left where you can pay what you like. Supposing they did that at restaurants, it would be chaos. It would depend what you thought of the meal I suppose. 'That was a five pound sermon' - or, 'Nothing today, Vicar'. I think he's going to start. Synchronise watches everyone.**

He looks at his wristwatch, his wife gives him an elbow.

PREACHER   *(Begins slowly with a pulpit voice)* My subject this morning is communication. Reaching out and making contact with people's hearts and minds. The prophet Isaiah said that the people cannot hear because their ears were heavy. He could have been speaking of today...

HUSBAND   *(Thinks)* **Isn't that strange. Heavy ears! I wonder how much an ear actually weighs. Being attached to us, we never really know. I read somewhere that the whole head can weigh several pounds - unbelievable.**

PREACHER   ...so the Gospel comes down to us through the pens of the Apostles, and the lives of the saints, and now it is in *our* hands. *(Thinks)* **I tremble to think of the Gospel being in the hands of some of them here.** *(He notices one of the congregation)* **There's Colonel Treater - He'll be down the pub and into his first pint before I've finished shaking hands with the congregation. Lord, I do wish you'd given me a more promising lot than this. I know, I know! Your twelve weren't all that likely. True. Goodness! There's Mrs Roper in the first pew - and with her husband, Now that's something! I think I'll smile at him. Make him feel welcome.**

It is in our hands to succeed or fail. What a challenge that is to all of us. *(He smiles at HUSBAND in the first row)*

HUSBAND   *(Thinks)* **Why does he keep looking at me? I'm sure he's looking at me. What about all the others? They need it more than me. Now he's smiling at me! What does that mean? What does he know about me, I wonder?**

PREACHER   So we must not remain silent. We must find ways to proclaim the Gospel - in the streets, in the workplace - from the housetops.

HUSBAND   *(Thinks)* **From the housetops! Now that would be a novelty!**

PREACHER   ...in season and out of season...

WIFE   *(Thinks)* **I knew there was something I needed. Tesco was out of seasoning. I wonder if that little shop on the corner would have some. It's no good sending *him*...**

She looks sideways at her husband who is gazing up at the PREACHER.

He'd forget his name if it wasn't on his credit card. Truth is we're both forgetting things these days. But he'd better not forget tomorrow - our Wedding Anniversary. He will, you see. He never even gets the year right. Thirty-five years. It hardly seems possible.

She gets out a tiny handkerchief and dabs her eyes. She nods to indicate the altar.

Just there it was. It seems like yesterday. 'For better, for worse.' Oh well! I wouldn't change anything. Not now. He's not perfect but then, neither am I - well, not absolutely.

She puts her handkerchief away, recovered.

HUSBAND	You all right, love?
WIFE	Oh, yes.
PREACHER	You may think that communicating is only for the clergy to do. Leave it to him I hear you say. He has received special training. He knows how to do it. People will listen to him, you say.
HUSBAND	*(Thinks)* **And, let's face it, he's got nothing else to do!**
PREACHER	But the truth is many people are put off by a clergyman. Oh, yes! What you say carries far more weight because you are *not* clergy. Think about that, wherever you will be tomorrow.
HUSBAND	*(Thinks)* **Tomorrow! Our Wedding Anniversary. I expect she thinks I've forgotten it. What a surprise she'll get when she comes down in the morning and sees the flowers, and the air tickets to Venice. Same hotel where we spent our honeymoon. Can't really afford it, but there you go. She deserves it, putting up with me for thirty-four years. Or is it thirty-five?**
PREACHER	Wherever you will be - there is your golden opportunity. Seize it, my friends - seize it. Ours is not just a Sunday Gospel, but for every day of the week. St Paul said, 'How shall they hear without a preacher?' There it is. The word is not heard till it is spoken, *(His voice rises)* and it is not seen till it is lived...
HUSBAND:	*(Thinks)* **Now he's off! He's enjoying himself. I hope he knows how to stop. Somebody really should speak to him about his hair. Perhaps he cuts it himself. Actually that is very hard to do**

	- cutting your own hair. Everything is the wrong way round. You could take an ear off. Oh dear! We're back to ears again!
PREACHER	Now I must hasten to my final thought.
HUSBAND	*(Thinks)* **Good.** ⎱
WIFE	*(Thinks)* **Good.** ⎰ *(Together)*
PREACHER	My final plea is simple. We must communicate. Talk to our friends, our acquaintances, our workmates, our neighbours. My friends, I ask you - is that so difficult?
	(Thinks) **It most certainly is! I never do it myself unless I'm on duty. Neither do they. Bob Peck there - he hasn't even spoken to his wife for years except to say 'Pass the salt' or 'Is it my turn to put the cat out?' Pathetic! Why, this lot even gets worried when I ask them to 'pass the Peace'.**
	...of course it isn't difficult! Just the right word at the right time and you will awaken people's desire to know more. So let me, if I may, leave it with you. Reach out. Make contact. Connect. Say the word, and the Gospel will take root and grow.
HUSBAND	Ten minutes exactly.
WIFE	Ssh!
PREACHER	Hymn number 80. 'How blessed are the feet'

All stand with hymnbooks open but do not mime singing.

WIFE	*(Thinks)* **I do hope my husband got something out of this service. I just hope he was listening and not up to his favourite occupation... day-dreaming.**
HUSBAND	*(Thinks)* **If the *Weekend Telegraph* has gone before I get to the newsagent, I shall bless that Vicar!**
WIFE	A - men. *(Sung)* ⎱
HUSBAND	A - men. *(Sung)* ⎰ *(Together)*

Quiet organ music as PREACHER goes to HUSBAND and WIFE.

PREACHER	Good morning, Mrs Roper.
WIFE	Good morning.
PREACHER	*And* you, Mr Roper. Good to see you.
HUSBAND	Good to see *you*, Vicar - and to hear you. Enjoyed your sermon. Yes. Specially that part about... er... well the er... you know, that bit about... er

WIFE	*(To the rescue)* About the importance of wedding anniversaries *(Looks at HUSBAND)* and remembering them.
PREACHER	Really? But I don't think I spoke about...
HUSBAND	And I liked that bit about 'leaving it with us'. That was good. Very good, Vicar. Very telling.
PREACHER	Thank you.
HUSBAND	By the way, what exactly was it you said you left with us?
PREACHER	If you'll excuse me, I must share myself with the congregation.
WIFE	Of course.

VICAR moves away to speak to others.

	Nice man, isn't he?
HUSBAND	Oh, yes. Now, I like somebody like that. You can see why he's popular. You can understand him. I mean, he gets through to you. As he said - that's what it's all about, after all. Making contact. Communication.
WIFE	Hurry up, dear.
HUSBAND	What?
WIFE	Get moving - now - quickly - or there's no way we'll be able to avoid talking to that awful Mrs Gosling.

They hurry off, followed at a more leisurely pace by the PREACHER, nodding and smiling to the congregation as he goes.

The sketch will repay careful rehearsal so that the card indicators are used smoothly and accurately, and during the 'Thinks' passages all those not speaking are concentrating on the PREACHER.

Talking Point

Do we try to conform to a role-model rather than being open with each other? How often do our thoughts not correspond with our deeds? How can we reconcile the two?

THE AGE OF THE COMPUTER

Production Note: *Four people are in line L to R. A and B are facing the audience, C and D have their backs to the audience. There is a small gap separating the two pairs.*

A	This is the age of the computer.
B	Speed.
A	Accuracy.
B	Capacity.
A	Some computers can perform millions of calculations a second.
B	And never get tired.
A	Computers can store the Bible, all the works of Shakespeare, all the great poets and philosophers, all the great encyclopaedias.
B	And never forget a line. They can perform complicated calculations of great difficulty. They always come up with the right answers.
A	And never boast about it. All this at your fingertips.
B	At the press of a button.
A	How much longer will we need books made of paper?
B	All the library space and miles of shelves?
A	Time-consuming searching?
B	What will happen to the guru and the teacher?
A	This is the age of the computer.
B	Shall we sit, isolated, in front of our monitors?
A	Confronted by limitless oceans of knowledge.
B	And dying of loneliness?

> *A and B now turn their backs to the audience at the same time as C and D turn to face the audience.*

C	This is the age of market forces.
D	Goods before people.
C	Profit before people.

D	Anything before people.
C	Who needs people?
D	Make it cheap and pile it high.
C	How long does it take to make?
D	Do it quicker.
C	How much does it cost?
D	Make it for less.
C	How big is your staff?
D	It's too many.
C	This is the age of cost management.
D	Get it right.
C	Or go under.
D	Who needs the shop assistant?
C	When we have the hypermarket?
D	Where is the little man who used to repair things?
C	If anything breaks, throw it away.
D	So what happened to the little man?
C	We threw him away.
D	Time is money.
C	Days are short.
D	Too short to pass the time of day.

> *C and D now turn their backs to the audience and A and B turn to the front again.*

A	This is the age of excitement.
B	Everything must make an impact.
A	If a thing's worth doing.
B	It's worth doing violently.
A	The video nasty nobody wants.
B	Is the video nasty that sells the best.
A	The illiterate obscenities that turned the air blue.
B	Now don't turn a hair.

> *In this one instance only, A turns to look at B to deliver the next line.*

A	But they're still obscene.
B	*(Very brief look at A)* Granted. An evening stroll alone in the park used to be a delight.

41

A	Now it's impossible.
B	The bobby on the street will soon be armed...
A	But no-one will know his name.
B	This is the age of excitement.
A	Turn up the disco volume.
B	Louder, I can still hear you.
A	The greatest commandment is...
B	Thou shalt not be bored.
A	And the second is this...
B	Thou shalt not be different, in case you find out who you are.

A and B remain facing front as C and D now also turn to the front.

C	This is an age of unbelief.
D	But not everywhere.
A	Fact: there are more Christians in the world today than in all the past ages put together.
B	Fact: in Asia, Latin America and Africa, many Churches are finding it hard to cope with new converts.
C	This is the age of mass communication.
D	So what are we saying to our generation?
A	The Gospel is the greatest news ever given to mankind.
B	That people are important.
C	And Christ is Saviour of the world.
D	Life can change.
A	And he can make it happen.
B	Rich and poor.
C	Black and white.
D	Male and female. Saint and sinner.
A	You and me.
B	His kingdom on earth has begun.
ALL	And nothing can stop it.

Talking Point

In the rapidly changing world of today, technology seems to call the tune. What is the place of humanity? Does God have a place?

JOHN THREE SOMETHING

Production Note: *A MAN is sitting on a park bench. He is not well dressed, but he is not a tramp. He is joined by a WOMAN who is carrying a shopping bag. She smiles at the seated man and sits at the other end of the bench. She produces a Bible from her bag. There is a moment of silence. The man looks briefly at the woman, then turns to the front again.*

MAN	Nice day.
WOMAN	*(Ecstatic)* Beautiful. Beautiful. *(Pause)* Psalm 118 verse 24.
MAN	*(Surprised)* Eh?
WOMAN	Psalm 118. 'This is the day the Lord has made. We will rejoice and be glad in it.'
MAN	*(Baffled but agreeing)* Oh, yes.
WOMAN	Verse 24.
MAN	*(Still baffled)* Right.

Pause.

WOMAN	*(Becomes poetic)* I come here to recharge my spirit. To feel the eternal rhythm of creation. Psalm 24 verse 1.
MAN	I come here to rest my feet.

Pause.

WOMAN	Spring is such a lovely time. 'The wilderness will rejoice and blossom, like the crocus it will burst into bloom.' Isaiah 35 verse1.
MAN	Not in *my* garden it won't. That really *is* a wilderness.

> *The MAN pulls out a paper bag and extracts a large, rough-cut sandwich. He offers the open bag to the WOMAN who declines with a puckered-up smile and a shake of the head. The MAN proceeds to eat.*

WOMAN	'This bread of ours was warm when we packed it at home, now see how mouldy it is.'

The MAN abruptly stops eating.

MAN	*(Incredulously)* That's not in the Bible!
WOMAN	*(Sweetly)* Yes it is. Joshua 9 verse 12.

She shows him the verse. He looks, then examines his sandwich.

MAN	*(Grumbling)* Made these me'self. Fresh this morning.

He takes another bite, but now isn't quite so sure about the taste.

WOMAN	Are you familiar with the Scriptures?
MAN	Oh, yes. You could say they're my life. In a manner of speaking.
WOMAN	Wonderful! 'How I love thy law. I meditate on it all day long.' Psalm 119 verse 97.
MAN	Amazing. You must have a very good memory.
WOMAN	I wouldn't say that.
MAN	You've been saying nothing else for the last five minutes. My trouble is I can't memorise anything.
WOMAN	'Remember the days of old, ask your father and he will tell you.'
MAN	No he won't - he's worse than me.
WOMAN	Deuteronomy 32 verse 6. *(Suddenly unsure)* No-o.
MAN	*(Mock alarm) Not* verse 6?
WOMAN	Verse 7. I think. Yes, that's it. Verse 7.
MAN	You had me worried there, for a minute!
WOMAN	A Christian who doesn't know his Bible is like a traveller without a map. Like a sailor without a chart. A messenger without a message. 'How shall they hear unless someone preach to them?' Romans 10 verse 14.

The MAN puts down his sandwich.

MAN   Do you mind? May I... ?

             He nods towards her Bible, which she willingly hands to him. He opens it and stabs a verse at random.

             2 Corinthians 9 verse 6.

             He challenges her with a questioning look.

WOMAN   'Whosoever sows sparingly will reap sparingly.'

             She is right. He tries again at random and stabs a page.

MAN   Matthew 7 verse 1.

             She knows this too, and smiles.

WOMAN   'Judge not, that ye be not judged.'

             Desperate, he stabs again elsewhere.

MAN   1 Chronicles 9 verse 39.

             He looks defiantly at her. She frowns darkly. He smiles as she wrestles with her memory.

             (Encouragingly, but slightly gloating) Well, you can't know everything.
WOMAN   Wait! 1 Chronicles 9 verse 39... 'and Ner was the father of Kish'.

             She beams. He checks, and she is right. He is disgruntled and hands back the Bible.

MAN   The Devil can quote Scripture to his advantage, you know. That's a proverb.
WOMAN   *(Eagerly)* Proverbs? Which chapter?

             She begins to look for it.

MAN	No, not in the Bible. It's just a proverb.
WOMAN	*(Shrugs)* I'm only interested in the Bible.

She clutches her Bible lovingly. The MAN comes forward with his paper bag and begins to throw crumbs to the birds.

MAN	*He* wasn't.
WOMAN	Who wasn't?
MAN	Him, of course. *(He nods upwards)* He wasn't just interested in the words. The way I see it, He loved *people* more than words.
WOMAN	Well, of course. People are important... but...
MAN	He would rather hear a man say 'sorry' to his neighbour than hear him recite any number of Psalms. That's what I think. Well, I must get back to work.

He screws up the paper bag and puts it in his pocket.

WOMAN	'For the night cometh wherein no man can work.' St John 9 verse 4.
MAN	You know - if we lost the Bible completely, with your memory I reckon we could get it all together again.
WOMAN	*(Flattered)* It's nice of you to say so, but *(Becomes demure)* 'We will not boast beyond proper limits.' 2 Corinthians 10 verse 13.

The MAN goes behind the bench and bends down to put on sandwich boards. Two placards are joined over the shoulders by straps.

MAN	You and I are both on the same side, you know.
WOMAN	'Praise the Lord.' Psalm 103 verse 1.

As he stands and faces us we see the words: 'For God so loved the world that He gave His only begotten Son.' He comes to the side of the bench R. The WOMAN looks at him in surprise.

MAN	In a manner of speaking.
WOMAN	What?
MAN	I began by wishing I had your memory, but I'm not so sure now. I

	wonder if He would approve, see.
WOMAN	Who?
MAN	*(Throws a glance upwards)* Him, of course!
WOMAN	Approve of what?

He walks off while speaking and we notice that the reference at the end of the text shows John 3 verse 15 with the number 15 crossed through and the number 16 put beside it.

MAN   Religion - by numbers.

He exits R. The WOMAN stands, and tucking her Bible firmly under her arm walks quickly off L.

This sketch is dedicated to all who cannot remember which books of the Bible come before and after Habakkuk.

Talking Point

What does it mean to know the Bible? What can we learn from the characters in this sketch?

Other Titles from RADIUS and NCEC

THE HILL
Sylvia Read
0-7197-0761-7

A modern mystery play in which the characters find themselves caught up in the experience of Easter. 30 mins.

Code No. PLA0761 (A)

CROSSTALK
Bob Irving
0-7197-0795-1

A collection of ten short plays based upon the parables which were, in their own time, sharp contemporary stories in an established tradition. In order to convey the same sense of immediacy these sketches are presented in a highly modern quick-firing style. No need for props or costumes, maximum cast of five. Each play lasts about 5 minutes.

Code No. PLA0795 (A)

SURPRISE SKETCHES
By Ronald Rich

SURPRISE SKETCHES
Ronald Rich
0-7197-0796-X

Five one-act plays with surprising endings. Ideal as a prompter for discussion or for use in worship, these plays examine some familiar human failings in a new stimulating style. Each play runs for about 10 minutes.

Code No. PLA0796 (A)

THE FLAME
Edmund Banyard
0-7197-0709-9

A novel approach to the idea of Pentecost, this play is a one act fantasy in the style of the Theatre of the Absurd. Four ordinary people are offered the 'Light of the World' by a messenger from the border between Time and Eternity. 25 mins.

Code No. FLA0709 (A)

> Performance times given are
> very approximate.

A FISTFUL OF FIVERS
Edmund Banyard
0-7197-0667-X

Twelve five-minute plays, each with a Christian message. Using the minimum of actors, scenery and props, these lively sketches will appeal to everyone who is young in the widest sense.

Code No. PLA0667 (A)

A FUNNY THING HAPPENED ON THE WAY TO JERICHO
Tom Long
0-7197-0722-6

The dress rehearsal for a presentation of the Good Samaritan turns out to be more than the leading player intended, as she is challenged by each of the roles she takes on in her search for the one she feels happy with. 30 mins.

Code No. FUN0722 (A) R

THE PRODIGAL DAUGHTER
William Fry
0-7197-0668-8

Using a neat twist, William Fry has turned one of the best-known parables into the tale of a present-day girl, updating the setting to portray some of the concerns of modern society. While it shows the seamier side of contemporary life, the message of this play is ultimately one of redemption and love. 30 mins.

Code No. PLA0668 (A)

NATIVITY LETTERS
Nick Warburton
0-7197-0724-2

Highlights the strains put on mother and daughter in the interdependence of a single parent family, which make them tend to disassociate themselves from other people. Help eventually presents itself through a committed teacher in the daughter's drama group. 40 mins.

Code No. NAT0724 (A)

WHO'LL BE BROTHER DONKEY?
Arthur Scholey
0-7197-0723-4

Three traditional Christmas tales are combined to produce this play where the animals use their Christmas Eve gift of speech to enact the crib scene in the hillside chapel. During the journey from their stable they outwit the wily Fox and Vixen in their malevolent schemes. The conclusion shows how the preparation of the crib scene is achieved against all odds through forgiveness of their fellow creatures and faith. 60 mins.

Code No. WHO0723 (A)